VERSES OF THE ETERNAL

"A POETIC EXPLORATION OF LOVE, SOLITUDE, AND NATURE"

DR. JIPSON LAWRANCE J

To the whispers of the wind,
the silent stars that watch over the night,
and the tender hearts that find solace in words—
This book is for you.

To those who have loved, lost, and learned,
and to the dreamers who keep hope alive,
I dedicate these verses,
with gratitude for the beauty and pain
that shape our souls.

May you find a piece of yourself
within these lines,
and may they light your way
through both the darkest nights
and the brightest days.

With all my love,

Dr. Jipson Lawrance Jaya

Contents

Contents

Contents

Foreword

In the vast and often tumultuous sea of literature, certain works stand out not merely for their content but for the depth of soul they reveal. My poetry collection is one such work—a luminous testament to the enduring power of words to heal, inspire, and transcend the ordinary.

This collection is more than a series of poems; it is a journey into the heart of the human experience. Through these verses, I have sought to weave intricate narratives that resonate deeply with readers, exploring the divine love of God, the quiet moments of solitude, and the raw emotions of heartbreak. Each poem is imbued with a profound sense of empathy and insight, inviting you to connect with the themes presented.

In these poems, I strive to connect the ancient with the modern, the spiritual with the secular, and the personal with the universal, reflecting my journey as both a poet and a thinker.

As you read this collection, you are not merely observing the world through my eyes; you are stepping into it, feeling the rhythms of nature, the weight of history, and the light of divine love. Each poem serves as a portal into a different aspect of life, inviting you to reflect, contemplate, and ultimately, deepen your understanding of yourself and the world around you.

My hope is that as you turn these pages, you will find solace in the beauty of the verses, strength in the exploration of struggles, and inspiration in the ever-present hope that I have sought to capture. This is a collection to be savored, revisited, and cherished—a true reflection of my soul and my desire to touch the hearts of those who read my work.

With deep sincerity and respect, I invite you to embark on this poetic journey, knowing that it will leave an indelible mark on your heart and mind, just as it has on mine.

Preface

The journey of creating this poetry collection has been one of deep introspection, exploration, and a sincere attempt to capture the essence of the human experience. As I bring this collection to you, it is with the hope that these verses will resonate with your own thoughts, emotions, and reflections.

From a young age, I have been captivated by the power of words—how they can convey the most complex emotions, paint vivid landscapes, and connect us to the deepest parts of ourselves and others. This collection is the culmination of years of contemplation, drawing inspiration from the world around me, the people I've encountered, and the experiences that have shaped my life.

In these poems, I explore themes of love, solitude, nature, and spiritual devotion, each one offering a different lens through which to view the world. Whether it's the quiet solace found in the embrace of nature, the pain and beauty of solitude, or the profound connections between the divine and the human, each poem is an invitation to pause, reflect, and engage with the deeper questions of life.

The blend of historical and mythological references within this collection serves to bridge the past with the present, offering a timeless perspective on the human condition. These narratives are not just relics of the past but living stories that continue to shape our understanding of ourselves and the world.

As you read through these pages, I encourage you to take your time, to immerse yourself in the emotions and imagery, and to allow the words to guide you on your own journey of discovery. This collection is not just a reflection of my thoughts and experiences, but a shared space where we can connect, understand, and find meaning together.

It is my sincere hope that these poems will inspire you, offer solace in times of need, and perhaps even challenge you to see the world in a new light. Poetry, for me, is a way to make sense of the world, to find beauty in the everyday, and to connect with something greater than ourselves. I invite you to explore this collection with an open heart and mind, and I hope that it will leave a lasting impression on you, just as it has on me during its creation.

Thank you for taking the time to engage with my work. It is my deepest wish that these poems will become a source of reflection, comfort, and inspiration for you.

Acknowledgements

The creation of this poetry collection has been a profound journey, and I am deeply grateful to those who have supported and inspired me along the way.

First and foremost, I would like to express my heartfelt thanks to my parents, Dr. D. E Lawrance and Mrs. Jaya Lawrance, whose unwavering love, guidance, and wisdom have shaped the person I am today. Their encouragement and belief in me have been the foundation upon which this work has been built. My father's dedication to healing and my mother's nurturing spirit have both been sources of deep inspiration.

To my elder brother, Mr. Lickson Lawrance, your constant support and encouragement have been invaluable. You have stood by me through every challenge, and your faith in my abilities has given me the strength to pursue my dreams.

I also wish to acknowledge my teachers, who have played a crucial role in my intellectual and creative development. Your guidance and mentorship have been instrumental in shaping my understanding of the world and my approach to writing. Special thanks to those who introduced me to the beauty of ancient languages and the depths of psychological exploration—your teachings have left an indelible mark on my work.

To my readers, your engagement with my poetry is the greatest reward I could ask for. It is your connection with these words that brings them to life, and I am deeply grateful for your time, attention, and thoughtful reflections.

I am also thankful to my friends and colleagues who have offered their insights, critiques, and encouragement throughout this journey. Your perspectives have enriched my work and pushed me to explore new dimensions in my writing.

Lastly, I would like to thank the countless poets, authors, and thinkers who have influenced my writing over the years. Your works have been a source of inspiration and a guiding light in my own creative endeavors.

This collection is a reflection of all the love, support, and inspiration I have received, and I am deeply thankful to everyone who has been a part of this journey.

Prologue

Poetry, at its core, is a dialogue between the soul and the world—a conversation that transcends time, space, and language. As you open this collection, you are not merely reading words on a page; you are stepping into a realm where emotions, thoughts, and experiences are distilled into their purest forms.

This collection was born out of a deep need to explore and understand the complexities of the human experience. It is an attempt to capture the fleeting moments of beauty, the quiet whispers of solitude, the intensity of love, and the profound connections that bind us to each other and the world around us. Each poem is a reflection of these moments, an effort to hold onto something ephemeral and give it form through language.

As you journey through these pages, you will encounter themes of love, both divine and human, the solace and challenges of solitude, the majesty of nature, and the intricate interplay between history, mythology, and the present. These poems are not confined to any one time or place; they are timeless explorations of the universal aspects of life that resonate with us all.

The prologue serves as an invitation—to pause, to breathe, and to immerse yourself in the world of these poems. Here, you will find stories that echo the struggles and triumphs of the human spirit, reflections that mirror your own thoughts and feelings, and verses that invite you to see the world through a different lens.

This is a space where the personal meets the universal, where individual experiences are woven into a larger tapestry of meaning. It is my hope that, as you read, you will find not only a connection to the words but also a deeper connection to yourself and the world around you.

Welcome to this journey of introspection and discovery. May these poems serve as companions on your own path, offering insight, comfort, and inspiration as you navigate the complexities of life. This is more than a collection of poetry; it is a reflection of the human experience in all its richness and diversity, and I am honored to share it with you.

1. "Sweeter Than Honey,"

In fields where wildflowers softly sway,
The bees hum low, then dart away,
Their journey begins at the break of day,
For nectar sweet, they'll work and play.
Golden sunlight, morning's rise,
Reflects in their industrious eyes,
They flit through blooms, under azure skies,
A symphony of wings that never lies.
Each petal kissed with tender grace,
A dance of love in nature's space,
Creating honey, a sweet embrace,
A gift from bees, nature's lace.
Honey drips like liquid gold,
A story ancient, yet retold,
In jars it's kept, a treasure bold,
Sweeter than honey, life's joy unfolds.
A taste of summer, pure and light,
Captured in a moment's flight,
From dawn's first blush to starry night,
Honey whispers sweet delight.
In every drop, a world unseen,
Of flowers, bees, and fields of green,
A testament to what has been,
Sweeter than honey, dreams serene.

2. Do I love God?

In the quiet moments, when the world is still,
I feel a presence, a gentle, loving will.
In the whispers of the wind, the rustling of the trees,
I sense a spirit, bringing me to my knees.
Your love, O God, is a beacon in the night,
Guiding me through shadows, to the morning light.
In the laughter of a child, in the kindness of a friend,
I see Your face, a love that has no end.
Your grace, a river, flowing ever free,
Washing over my soul, setting me to be.
In the trials and tribulations, in the joy and the pain,
I find Your presence, in every drop of rain.
With every breath, I take, with every beat of my heart,
I feel Your love, never to depart.
In the depths of my soul, in the heights above,
I know the truth: yes, I love God.

3. The Solitude's Whisper

In the silent echo of the night,
Where shadows dance with fading light,
A heart's soft whisper, barely heard,
Loneliness weaves its mournful word.
Through empty halls, it gently creeps,
In quiet corners, secrets keeps,
A hollow ache, a silent cry,
Beneath the moon's indifferent eye.
A solitude that's deep and vast,
Where memories of the past hold fast,
A whisper soft, a sigh profound,
In this lonely, aching sound.
Yet in the dark, a spark may glow,
A seed of hope, a chance to grow,
For in the depths of lonely night,
The heart may find its own true light.
So hold on tight, through shadows deep,
In sorrow's grasp, do not weep,
For dawn will break, and with it bring,
A melody that hearts may sing.
In the stillness, strength is found,
In quiet whispers, love's sweet sound,
Loneliness may have its part,
But it cannot claim a steadfast heart.

4. Loneliness That Broke the Heart

In the stillness of a night so deep,
Where shadows dance and silence weep,
There lies a heart, once full of light,
Now burdened by the endless night.
Once it beat with rhythm true,
With joy and love, and skies so blue,
But time and fate, they played their part,
And loneliness, it broke the heart.
In halls where laughter used to ring,
Where joy was found in everything,
Now echoes only hollow sound,
A lonely heart, by sorrow bound.
The friends have faded, drifted far,
Like whispers lost among the stars,
And in their place, a void so vast,
A lonely heart, a broken past.
The days are long, the nights are cold,
No tender hand, no love to hold,
Just memories of times gone by,
And tears that fall from weary eyes.
The world moves on, in endless spin,
Yet here I am, trapped deep within,

A cage of thoughts, a prison stark,
Loneliness that broke the heart.
Yet in the dark, a spark remains,
A tiny hope amid the pains,
That somewhere in this vast expanse,
There lies a chance for one more dance.
A dance of love, of healing grace,
To mend the heart, to find its place,
In arms that hold, in love so true,
To chase away this shade of blue.
For even in the darkest night,
There lies a path to morning light,
A heart once broken, can repair,
With love, with hope, with tender care.
So let the tears fall where they may,
And let the sorrow have its say,
But know that even in the dark,
There lies the spark to heal the heart.
For loneliness may break us down,
But in its wake, we can be found,
With strength to rise, to love anew,
And build a heart both strong and true.

5. A Home Where Love Blooms

In a home where love blooms, soft and bright,
Every room whispers tales of pure delight.
Sunlight streams through windows, warm and wide,
Filling each corner with a golden tide.
Walls adorned with laughter's sweet refrain,
Echoes of joy that forever remain.
Soft whispers shared in the calm of night,
Dreams take flight in the tender light.
The kitchen fills with aromas divine,
Love stirred into every line.
Meals are shared with hearts so near,
Creating memories we hold dear.
In the living room, stories unfold,
Of days gone by and secrets retold.
Couches worn by countless sighs,
Witness to love that never dies.
The garden blooms in colors grand,
Tended by a gentle hand.
Flowers sway to the breeze's song,
A testament to love, lifelong.
Bedrooms cradle restful dreams,
Wrapped in love's warm, soothing beams.

Pillows hear the quiet prayers,
Of hopes and wishes, love's affairs.
A home where love blooms is a place,
Where hearts find peace and gentle grace.
In every corner, love resides,
A sanctuary where it abides.

6. "The Lamp's Farewell"

The wind extinguished the lamp,
A flicker's last breath, a faint clamp.
Darkness wrapped the room in its shawl,
Whispering secrets, silencing all.
The flame danced bravely in the breeze,
A delicate waltz, a tease.
But the wind, with its cold, unseen hand,
Erased its light, reclaiming the land.
Shadows crept in, filling the space,
An eerie stillness took its place.
Yet in the dark, a quiet calm,
A night's embrace, a soothing balm.
Stars outside began to gleam,
Softly casting a silver dream.
Though the lamp's glow was no more,
The night sang its ancient lore.
The wind extinguished the lamp, it's true,
But it lit up the skies anew.
In every end, a new start,
A silent echo in the heart.

7. Wipes My Unseen Tears

In the silence of the night,
Where shadows softly blend,
A whisper finds the light,
As unseen tears descend.
A gentle touch, a tender care,
From hands that know no bounds,
Wipes away my hidden despair,
In solace, peace is found.
Through the veil of sorrow's haze,
A beacon bright appears,
Guiding me through troubled days,
Wiping unseen tears.
In the quiet, in the still,
Where pain and hope collide,
A heart that understands my will,
Stands steadfast by my side.
No need for words, no need for cries,
Just presence, pure and clear,
Wipes my tears, unseen by eyes,
And brings my soul near.
In every tear that's wiped away,
A strength begins to bloom,
Turning night into the day,
Dispelling all the gloom.

So here I stand, renewed, reborn,
With courage that perseveres,
For love has come, both soft and warm,
And wiped my unseen tears.

8. "Echoes of a Broken Soul"

In the silent night, beneath the moon's soft glow,
A man sits alone, where the shadows grow.
His heart is heavy, a storm within his chest,
A mind in turmoil, longing for rest.
His dreams once vibrant, now faded and torn,
In the echoes of time, his spirit is worn.
Philosophical questions, a labyrinth of thought,
In the depths of his soul, he feels overwrought.
He seeks the meaning in the vast, starry sky,
Why does one live, and why must one die?
The answers elude him, like whispers in the breeze,
Leaving him stranded, alone with his pleas.
He ponders existence, the purpose of pain,
Why joy must be fleeting, like drops of rain.
Each dawn brings new light, yet he remains in the dark,
A wanderer lost, without a spark.
Memories haunt him, like ghosts in the night,
Regrets and missed chances, out of his sight.
His heart aches with sorrow, a deep, endless well,
In the silence, his secrets he'll never tell.
Yet in his despair, there's a flicker of hope,
A distant horizon, a shimmering slope.
For in every question, in every tear,
Lies the essence of life, both fragile and dear.

He may be broken, his path unclear,
But in his journey, he confronts his fear.
For in the struggle, there's beauty profound,
In the darkest of places, light can be found.
So he rises once more, with a heart worn and scarred,
Embracing the journey, though it may be hard.
For the deeply broken, philosophically stuck,
Are the souls that remind us to never give up.

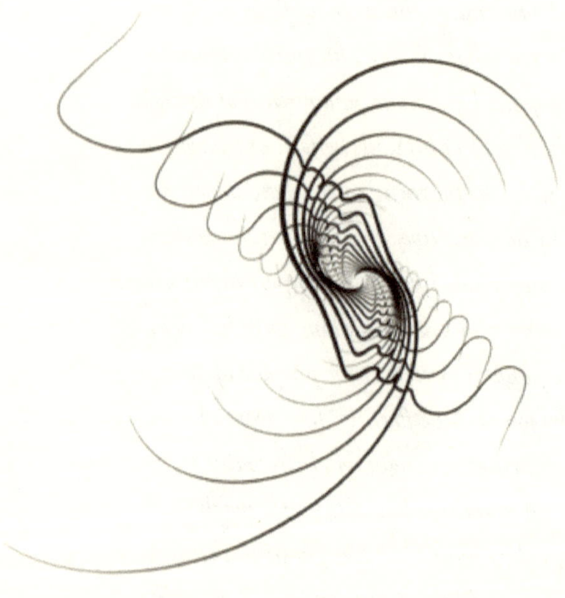

9. A Solitary Flower in the Temple

In the temple's quiet hush,
Amid the sacred, silent crush,
A solitary bloom does dwell,
Its beauty casts a subtle spell.
Petals soft in colors bright,
Gentle glow in soft moonlight,
Amidst the stone, so cold and gray,
The flower's grace does gently sway.
In the sacred, hallowed air,
Perfume rises, pure and rare,
A single bloom, a soul's delight,
In temple's heart, a gentle light.
Alone it stands, yet not unseen,
A symbol of what life can mean,
In solitude, in quiet power,
A temple's heart, a single flower.

10. Rule My Land

Rise with honor, lead with grace,
United hearts, a strong embrace,
Loyalty to justice, hand in hand,
Ever steadfast, we rule our land.
Majesty in every stride,
Yearn for peace, with truth as guide,
Luminous paths, together we stand,
Aspire to greatness, across the land,
Never falter, never bend,
Defend our home, till the very end.

11. The Man Who Hates the Rose

The man who hates the rose has eyes so cold,
He shuns the bloom with fervor and disdain,
In gardens where the petals do unfold.
His heart, once warm, now feels so old,
He walks alone, avoiding beauty's chain,
The man who hates the rose has eyes so cold.
He tells of thorns and tales of love untold,
Of passion lost in sorrow's heavy rain,
In gardens where the petals do unfold.
Where others see a treasure to behold,
He sees the pain, the hurt, the endless strain,
The man who hates the rose has eyes so cold.
Yet in his mind, a memory does scold,
A fleeting glimpse of joy he can't regain,
In gardens where the petals do unfold.
Perhaps one day his heart will break the mold,
And learn to love the rose despite the pain,
The man who hates the rose has eyes so cold,
In gardens where the petals do unfold.

12. The Loom of Night

In the quiet realm where twilight weaves,
A darkness unfurls its ancient sleeves,
Threads of shadow, deep and vast,
Unravelling moments of the day long past.
Stars emerge, like scattered seeds,
Sown in the fabric of cosmic deeds,
Each one a beacon, a distant song,
Guiding the lost where they belong.
The moon, a silver needle in the night,
Stitches through the dark with gentle light,
Casting patterns on the silent land,
Weaving dreams with a delicate hand.
In this vast and endless tapestry,
Secrets whisper in the midnight breeze,
Stories of ages, both lost and found,
In the velvet dark where echoes sound.
Mysteries bloom in the deepening shade,
Where the light of day begins to fade,
The heart of night holds tales untold,
In its endless expanse, both fierce and bold.
As shadows dance and softly blend,
The edges of the world transcend,
A place where fears and hopes entwine,
In the loom of night, a grand design.

The darkness deepens, yet so serene,
A canvas where all dreams convene,
A realm where time itself stands still,
And every thought can bend to will.
Embrace the night, let go of day,
For in the darkness, we find our way,
In the tangled threads of the cosmic scheme,
The loom of night crafts every dream.
So let the shadows weave their art,
Their threads are a reflection of the heart,
In the endless weave of night's domain,
Where the darkness unravels, yet remains.

13. The Golden Touch

In ancient lands where tales unfold,
King Midas ruled with heart of gold,
A Satyr's favor won him grace,
A wish for gold, he did embrace.
"Let all I touch turn to gold," he cried,
Though warned by Dionysus, who tried
To curb his greed with words so wise,
But Midas' heart was set on prize.
With joy he touched the common things,
And soon his world was gilded bling,
Yet hunger struck with cruel decree,
For gold can't feed nor set one free.
His daughter came with love's embrace,
But turned to gold in her father's space,
The joy of wealth turned to despair,
As golden touch brought sorrow rare.
He learned too late, as gold did gleam,
That greed can shatter every dream,
The riches he had yearned to hold,
Now left him cold and very old.
So heed this tale of Midas' plight,
Where greed turns gold to hollow light,
For true wealth lies not in gleaming might,
But in love and joy, pure and bright.

14. "The Elephant's Triumph: A Forest's True Friend"

In the heart of the forest, so lush and so green,
Lived a lonely old elephant, kind and serene.
He roamed through the meadows, and walked through the glade,
Hoping for friends, but the forest was staid.
A monkey swung high from a vine in the trees,
With a flick of its tail and a swing in the breeze.
"I can't be your friend," said the monkey with glee,
"For you cannot swing high like me in the trees."
A rabbit so swift with a hop and a bound,
In a burrow so tiny, so snug and so round.
"It's quite clear," said the rabbit, "you're far too grand,
For my burrow so small, you'd not fit in the land."
A frog by the pond with a leap and a splash,
Saw the elephant large with a tremor and crash.
"You can't jump like I do," the frog croaked with a sigh,
"So I can't be your friend, though I don't mean to pry."
The tiger then roared with a fearsome display,
Scaring the creatures who scattered away.
The elephant heard all the cries and the shouts,
And decided to find what the trouble was about.

He met a bear, trembling, shaking with fright,
Who told of the tiger's fierce, terrible might.
With courage, the elephant ambled on through,
To confront the great tiger with a heart brave and true.
"Please stop," said the elephant, voice gentle but firm,
"Your fierce roar and growl are causing concern."
The tiger just sneered, "Stay out of my way,"
But the elephant kicked and sent it away.
The tiger fled fast, and the forest was calm,
The creatures emerged, their hearts now with balm.
They looked at the elephant, large and so grand,
And saw in his size a protector so grand.
"Dear elephant," they said with voices so bright,
"You've proven your worth in this perilous fight.
We see now the strength and the courage you bring,
And welcome you here as a friend, a true king."
So the forest now echoed with laughter and cheer,
For the lonely old elephant now had friends near.
With a heart full of joy and a soul ever kind,
The elephant's friendships were the best you could find.

15. "Threads of Fate"

In ancient threads, a tale was spun,
Of Oedipus, whose fate was done.
A king, a prince, in myth's embrace,
Who sought to change his destined place.
The Moirai, with their weaving hand,
Had charted out a future grand.
No mortal power, nor divine,
Could shift the threads of fate's design.
King Laius, with his heart defied,
Fled from his fate, with hope belied.
And Oedipus, with courage grand,
Sought to escape fate's heavy hand.
Yet, in their flight from what was known,
They met their end, as fate had shown.
No god or man could alter the course,
Of destiny's unyielding force.
In tragedy, their stories blend,
A lesson clear: no fate can mend.
To run from fate is but a pain,
For what is meant will still remain.

16. Flight of Icarus

In a tower tall, where shadows play,
A father's words began to weigh,
"Beware the sun, its fiery gaze,
For wax and feathers will betray."
Yet youth, so bold, with dreams alight,
Touched by the golden rays of might,
His wings of wax, in sunlight warm,
Defied the warning, braved the storm.
To heights unknown, his heart did soar,
Unfettered by the tales of yore,
He felt the heat, the sun's embrace,
And dared to challenge nature's grace.
The melting wax, a tragic sign,
As pride and recklessness align,
The sky, once vast, now turned to doom,
His flight reduced to mournful gloom.
In waters deep, where dreams descend,
A lesson learned, too late to mend,
For Icarus, in reckless flight,
Found wisdom in the depths of night.
So heed the tale of pride and fire,
Of wings that melt and dreams that tire,
For in the sun's relentless blaze,
Lie perils for the bold who daze.

17. "The Rise of Zeus: The Thunderer's Triumph"

(Based on Greek myth)
In ancient times, where legends tread,
A tale of gods and power spread,
Of Zeus, the king with thunder's roar,
Who soared above the Titan lore.
Born of Cronus, feared and grim,
Who swallowed children on a whim,
Zeus' fate was forged in shadows deep,
Yet in the dark, his hope did sleep.
Rhea, wise, with cunning swift,
Wrapped a stone in a deceitful gift,
And hid her son in Crete's embrace,
Where nymphs and Curetes kept their pace.
Amongst the gods, his strength did grow,
A force to fear, a mighty show,
He led the charge with lightning's flare,
To challenge Titans, lay them bare.
Titanomachy, the war of skies,
Where gods and titans met their ties,
Zeus rose victorious, fierce and bright,
To claim his throne in divine light.
So legends tell of thunder's might,

Of Zeus, who brought the dawn from night,
His tale is one of strength and will,
A god who stands supreme, still.

18. "Serenade of the Starlit Night"

In the heart's quiet glen, where echoes softly play,
Gentle breezes weave through twilight's soft ballet.
Stars peek from their veils, and the moon's tender gaze,
Casts a silver glow on the midnight's quiet praise.
Amidst the deodar's whisper and the night's tender hue,
A melody stirs, as if ancient dreams renew.
A chariot of starlight, with celestial grace,
Brings forth a presence, with a timeless embrace.
My muse, my serenade, in the night's gentle stream,
Wears the robe of moonlight, and dances in a dream.
Her voice, a cascade of melodies divine,
Sings the language of stardust, in a rhythm so fine.
In the garden of silence, where the night blooms serene,
She paints the dark canvas with a symphony unseen.
With each note, a whisper, each chord, a caress,
She brings to the stillness a sublime tenderness.
In this sacred hush, where night and music entwine,
Her song is the beacon, a celestial sign.
Through the twilight and shadows, her voice softly glows,
Guiding hearts through the night, where true beauty flows.

19. "Symphony of the Heart"

In the garden of twilight dreams,
Where moonlight gently streams,
A melody whispers through the air,
An ode to love, beyond compare.
In the vault of starlit skies,
Where secrets and wonder lie,
You'll find the echoes of my soul,
A serenade, both tender and whole.
Glimmers of affection shine bright,
In the shadowed depths of night,
A symphony of joy and grace,
Dancing softly in this sacred space.
You hold the key to my heart's gate,
A jewel that time cannot abate,
A realm where every note is pure,
A dance of love that will endure.
So, if you seek a love so grand,
In the garden where dreams expand,
Come and listen, come and see,
The song of my heart, eternally.

20. Whispers of a Gentle Dawn

In the hush of dawn's embrace,
The sky unfolds its velvet grace,
A tender hue of calm delight,
Where dreams take flight in soft twilight.
The air, adorned with fragrant hints,
Sings with a melody that glints,
In every breath, a whispered song,
Where tranquil moments drift along.
Beneath the heavens' quiet sweep,
In stillness deep, where shadows sleep,
The soul finds rest in nature's calm,
Wrapped in the serenity's balm.
The early light, with gentle hand,
Paints the day in shades so grand,
Like petals soft, and breezes mild,
Each moment feels divinely styled.
As days unfold with subtle change,
And colors dance in hues estranged,
A peaceful hush begins to spread,
Where warmth and grace are gently led.
In this embrace of quiet light,
Where spring and stillness unite,

The heart is cradled, pure and true,
In the tender dawn's embrace of blue.

21. The Illuminator: The Life and Legacy of Thomas Alva Edison

In Milan, Ohio, a boy was born,
With dreams and ideas that couldn't be torn.
Thomas Alva Edison, his name would shine,
A beacon of brilliance through the sands of time.
With little schooling, but a curious mind,
In his father's basement, discoveries he'd find.
At ten, a laboratory, experiments would start,
At twelve, on trains, he sold with a heart.
A telegrapher by trade in his early years,
Through Morse code clicks, he conquered fears.
Partial deafness, a challenge he knew,
But innovation's fire in his soul fiercely grew.
For Western Union, he crafted with skill,
A machine for messages, an invention of will.
Sold to a rival for a hundred grand,
A testament to the brilliance of his hand.
Menlo Park, a haven for dreams to spark,
There he created in the dark.
A carbon-button transmitter, a phonograph's sound,
The incandescent lightbulb, shining all around.

Financiers like Morgan and Vanderbilts gave,
Thirty thousand dollars, for the light to pave.
In Manhattan's heart, the power began,
The world's first system, lit by this man.
His first wife passed, sorrow did follow,
To West Orange, he moved, with dreams not hollow.
A new lab he built, phonograph to thrive,
Motion pictures, new stories to contrive.
An alkaline battery, energy stored,
Edison's mind, forever soared.
His later years, quieter but bright,
Invention his purpose, his guiding light.
With 1,093 patents, a record unmatched,
Nearly 400 for light, his legacy attached.
He invented for necessity, new paths to carve,
The modern electric world, from his vision did starve.
Thomas Alva Edison, a name to revere,
A man of innovation, undeterred by fear.
Through decades of work, his brilliance unfurled,
He laid the foundation for our electrified world.

22. A Little Bird's Tale

Oh tiny bird, with wings so free,
Are your days just endless glee?
No dark clouds or storms to face,
Do you learn to fly with grace?
Perched on branches, high and bright,
You sing with joy, take flight in light,
Soaring high with boundless cheer,
Could I ever do that here?
On my swing, I sway and dream,
Feeling light, a playful gleam,
You, dear bird, touch skies so blue,
How do you embrace such hue?
Across the hills and rivers wide,
You paint the world with every glide,
Roosting bold on beasts so grand,
Your adventures, vast and unplanned.
Oh, celestial being of the skies,
Your freedom tempts and mesmerizes,
I sit with books, my mind confined,
Wishing I could leave it all behind.
Why wasn't I a bird so small,
With wings to rise above it all?
To dance with winds and chase the sun,
A life of joy, forever fun.

23. Beacon of Integrity

Amidst the dimming lights of valor,
Glowing truths, like stars, retreat,
Virtue falters in its armor,
While deceit gains ground, replete.
Justice, once a guiding beacon,
Fades beneath the storm's advance,
Human warmth, in shadows weakened,
Gives way to a darker dance.
Honesty, now rare and fleeting,
Succumbs to whispers of the sly,
Trust and faith in silence meeting,
Beneath a cold and watchful sky.
Yet within the heart's deep chamber,
Burns a flame that won't relent,
In the face of looming danger,
It stands firm, though world be bent.
For every act of silent courage,
Each small truth upheld with pride,
Grows a light to pierce the darkness,
And turn the tide of time's great tide.
Hold fast, let virtue be your anchor,
Amidst the waves of doubt and scorn,
For in the end, through trial's rancor,
Integrity shall be reborn.

No falsehoods shall defeat the righteous,
No shadows dim the pure of heart,
For in the soul's enduring brightness,
Lies the strength to never part.

24. Ethereal Blossom

In the garden's tender embrace,
A fragrance pure and sweet does rise,
Unfolding whispers of a dove,
Soft petals bloom beneath the skies.
Among the leaves of emerald green,
A virgin bloom of white appears,
Like pearls strung in the morning light,
Reflecting love, dissolving fears.
Is it a star fallen from above?
Or dew-kissed silk with scent divine?
A shell from ocean's secret depths,
In perfect form, its edges fine.
Such artistry in nature's hand,
A masterpiece in fragile grace,
No earthly beauty can compare,
The dove-flower holds a sacred place.
Behold the gentle dove within,
So pure, serene, and soft its flight,
A symbol of the soul's own quest,
For truth and love, for peace and light.
O flower of the dove's own hue,
With silent songs and gentle charm,
You teach the heart to dream and hope,
To seek the shelter of your calm.

Unbound by worldly knowledge vast,
Untouched by wisdom's endless chase,
You speak the language of the heart,
In every petal, love we trace.
Dove-flower, sacred, softly speak,
Of mysteries, the soul has missed,
Guide us with your tender glow,
To realms where love and light persist.

25. Whispers of November

Amidst the waiting Jasmine's quiet dusk,
Bloomless and silent, it faded to musk.
Hopes in fragments, in boats adrift,
Journeys untravelled, a heart to lift.
The winds grew fierce, a soul unseen,
Becoming no one, where strength has been.
Winged warmth of love songs true,
Parrots' serenade in skies of blue.
Yet they depart, in search of dreams,
Nests abandoned, in silence screams.
A lion's roar in a sudden blaze,
Life's rented door, in ashen haze.
Paid in full, the debts of sorrow,
Memory's knot, a key for tomorrow.
As dawn unveiled the wedding's fire,
A heart burned bright with unquenched desire.
On wormwood's branch, the crows convene,
Under rain's weight, hope's fragile scene.
Shattered fish in downpour's might,
Picture booths fell, no respite.
In the embrace of silent pain,
Tears withheld, yet not in vain.
Alone, I walked November's Road,
Embracing sorrow, my heart's abode.

26. The Awakening of the Rough Beast

In the whirling void of ancient lore,
The eagle's cry no longer hears the shore;
Chaos reigns, and harmony's thread is torn,
Unleashing darkness from the light once sworn.
Blood-red waves engulf the sacred rites,
Innocence is drowned in endless nights;
The noble heart is seized by silent doubt,
While fervent frenzy fills the air without.
Surely a vision breaks the midnight haze;
Surely a prophecy ignites the blaze.
The second dawn! From realms of unseen dread,
A phantom stirs, born of the cosmic thread.
Amidst the dunes, where time and space collide,
A beast with human face and leonine stride,
Eyes void of mercy, glaring like the sun,
Moves forth with limbs of ancient burdens spun.
The vultures' shadows circle in dismay,
As darkness falls, eclipsing the new day.
Centuries of slumber churn to wake,
Disturbed by whispers that the cradle shakes.
What monstrous specter, with intent unchaste,
Lumbers toward Bethlehem with ominous haste?

A creature forged from humankind's despair,
A herald of an epoch's end, laid bare.
Its coming marks the twilight of our reign,
In shadows, hope and dread entwined, remain.
Yet in this hour of dread and shifting sands,
The truth emerges from celestial hands:
Within the beast, a spark of light concealed,
A path to redemption yet unsealed.
For as the world descends in ceaseless strife,
There lies within the chaos, seeds of life.
From crumbling ruins, new worlds are reborn,
And from the darkest night, springs forth the dawn.

27. Whisper of the Forest

My heart beats heavy, and a silent shiver creeps
Through my veins, as if a shadowed spell has bound,
Or a somber nightingale sings me to sleeps,
In moonlit forests where no sorrows are found:
Not for envy of thy serene flight,
But longing to share in thy pure delight,
O spirit of the twilight trees,
In mystic glades,
Where emerald leaves and twilight's gentle breeze,
Whisper of peace in evening's tender shades.
O for a sip of timeless, starry wine,
That's hidden deep in ancient, sacred groves,
Savoring the mystique of earth's divine,
Dance of whispers, and the soft embrace of cloves!
O for a chalice brimming with the night,
Full of dreams, and twilight's serene song,
With twinkling stars that kiss the silent height,
And twilight's dusky throng;
That I might drink, and slip away unseen,
And with thee, glide through shadows evergreen:
Drift far away, dissolve into the mist,
Where thou, in leafy bowers, art ever blest,
Where the weary heart can rest,
Here, where the mortal struggle never ceases,

Where dreams are shattered, and hope decreases;
Where beauty fades and love is left to pine,
Where but to feel is to be bound in sorrow,
And night falls heavy as each morrow.
Fly! O fly! For I will soar with thee,
Not borne by earthly toils or mortal chains,
But on the ethereal wings of reverie,
Though my spirit faints and mind refrains:
With thee already! tender is the night,
And perhaps the stars twinkle with delight,
Surrounded by whispers of the past;
But here, the darkness wraps tight,
Save for what heaven sends through breezy gusts
In lush shadows and winding, ancient paths.
I cannot see the blossoms at my feet,
Nor what fragrant scents drift on the air,
But in the sacred dark, each secret sweet
Whispers its presence with a tender care
To the glades, the thicket, and the wild orchard;
White blossoms, and the gentle eglantine;
Fading violets hidden in the dusk;
And midsummer's child,
The rising moonflower, full of midnight's musk,
The quiet haven of stars on tranquil eves.
Listening, I drift; and, for many times
I have felt a love for silent Night,
Called it a friend in many whispered rhymes,
To carry me away on wings of light;
Now, more than ever, seems it rich to dream,

To fade into the starlight without pain,
While thou art singing, pouring forth thy soul
In such pure harmony!
Still wouldst thou sing, and I would hear in vain—
To thy eternal song become a part.
Thou art immortal, spirit of the night!
No passing age can wear thee down;
The voice I hear this gentle night was heard
In ancient times by wise and lost:
Perhaps the very tune that soothed
The wanderer Ruth, when longing for her home,
She stood in fields of distant lands;
The same that often charmed
Mystic windows, opening to the sea
Of unknown realms, in enchanted lands forlorn.
Forlorn! the very word pulls me from thee
Back to my solemn self!
Goodbye! The dream cannot deceive as well
As it is famed to do, a fanciful sprite.
Bye-bye! thy tender hymn fades
Beyond the quiet meadows, over the still stream,
Up the hillside; and now it's lost
In the distant valleys deep:
Was it a vision, or a waking dream?
Gone is that music: —Do I wake or sleep?

28. Behind the Veil

We don the veil that cloaks our fears,
A shroud that muffles cries and tears.
This cost we bear for calm disguise;
With weary hearts, our hopes we guise,
And navigate through tangled lies.
Why should the world discern our pain,
In every smile, the hidden strain?
Verily, let them see the polished face,
We don the veil.
We laugh, but oh, our spirits wail,
To heavens high, our pleas set sail.
We dance, but oh, the ground is cold
Beneath our steps, the path is old;
But let the world believe the tale,
We don the veil.
With silent screams, our truths we hide,
In shadows deep, our griefs abide.
This burdened guise, a daily task,
Yet still we wear the hollow mask.
For in the dark, our sorrows swell,
But let the world dream sweet as well,
We don the veil.

29. Faith's Answer

Beyond the cycles of each season's dance,
Where time's slow passage grants us no advance,
Beyond the tears cascading down our face,
Remember too the smiles that interlace.
When gazing up to God with hopeful eyes,
Know answers come beneath His vast, clear skies.
Though past may pain, and tears may often fall,
Sweet healing's balm will soothe and mend us all.
Beyond the darkest clouds that mar the sky,
There lies a brilliance where the sun is high.
In faith, when we to God extend our hand,
Assured, His answers meet our every strand.
Though nights be long and shrouded in their gloom,
The dawn breaks forth with bright, resplendent bloom.
Indignation's wave may surge and swell,
Yet peace from God will in our hearts dwell.
In faith, we cast our cares into His grace,
For every question finds its rightful place.
Beyond each trial, in faith we seek His call,
Assured that He will answer, guiding all.

30. Indignation

In the quiet heart of night,
Where shadows dare to tread,
Rises indignation's might,
A flame in hearts long bled.
With a voice like thunder's roar,
It shatters chains unseen,
For justice, it implores,
In realms both fierce and serene.
Eyes ablaze with righteous fire,
It stands, unbowed, unbent,
Against the tides of dark desire,
A force, fierce and unspent.
No tyranny can quell its blaze,
Nor silence it with fear,
For indignation's fervent gaze,
Holds truths both sharp and clear.
In every pulse, it finds its beat,
Injustice fuels its cry,
A testament to those who meet
Oppression eye to eye.
So let its fervor guide the lost,
And kindle hearts grown cold,
For indignation bears the cost,
Of freedom, bright and bold.

31. Ode to Woe

In the shadowed vale where echoes flow,
A solemn word does softly grow,
With every breath, with every sigh,
It weaves a tale, it whispers, "Woe."
Beneath the moon's ethereal glow,
In lands where sorrow's winds do blow,
The heart does ache, the spirit bends,
And life becomes a mournful show.
Oh woe, thou art a weighty chain,
A spectral hand, a dark refrain,
Thou lingerest in the quiet night,
And paintest skies with tears of rain.
In every drop of sorrow's dew,
Thy presence felt, thy essence true,
Yet in thy depths, a strength resides,
A fire that life does then renew.
For woe doth teach the heart to see,
The beauty in the misery,
A tender touch, a gentle word,
In pain, we find our empathy.
So sing, oh woe, thy haunting song,
For in thy chords, we grow so strong,
Through trials faced, and tears once shed,
We rise anew, where we belong.

In the dance of shadows, light does gleam,
And woe becomes a distant dream,
For from the darkness, dawn does break,
And in its light, we find our theme.

32. A Whisper in the Wind

If fate decrees we shan't entwine in this life's fleeting span,
Let me always sense the absence of your visage in my mind's panorama.
May this longing be my constant companion, an echo in my heart,
In dreams where shadows linger, and in the bright of day, never apart.
As I traverse the bustling streets, hands laden with transient gains,
Let me feel the hollow of these riches, a wealth that only feigns.
Let the ache of your absence be the silent song I sing,
In every wakeful moment, in every dusk and dawn, a persistent sting.
When I rest upon the weary path, breathless and worn,
When the dust becomes my solace, my journey far from shorn,
May the distance yet to travel be the compass of my soul,
A reminder of the road that stretches to an unattainable goal.
In the midst of merry gatherings, where joy and mirth abound,
Let the emptiness of your absence in my heart resound.
Though my halls be filled with music and laughter rich and clear,
Let me always feel the void, knowing you are not near.
Oh, let this sorrow be the thread that weaves through all my days,
A constant, gentle torment in a thousand subtle ways.
For in this longing, I find a truth that no mirage can sever,
That in missing you, beloved, I am yours forever.

33. The Tireless Wheel

In fields of toil, a soul was born,
A tireless wheel through night and morn.
His life was motion, never still,
A heart of steel, unyielding will.
He spun and whirred, a ceaseless clock,
Purpose clear, a steady rock.
Within his rhythm, life did bloom,
A constant pulse that chased the gloom.
He forged a world of gears and grind,
A dynamo of body and mind.
Conquering fears with every turn,
In work's embrace, his passions burned.
A vibrant sound, a whirring grace,
In motion's dance, he found his place.
But time, the silent, creeping thief,
Brought wear and tear, a hidden grief.
The grease that kept his fervor bright,
Was stolen by the quiet night.
His parts grew stiff, his speed reduced,
A whisper where once thunder loosed.
He strained to move, to find his beat,
But gears once fluid, now concrete.
He yearned for tasks to fill his days,
For burdens strong to light his ways.

In idleness, a heavy weight,
An emptiness that sealed his fate.
He cried for work, a labor true,
To keep him moving, through and through.
For in the stillness, doom he found,
A final silence, heart unbound.
His life of motion, now a ghost,
A tireless spirit missed the most.
So mourn him now, this noble soul,
Whose life was motion, whose end was whole.
A dancer in the gears of fate,
Whose heart beat strong, whose work was great.
In his rest, a tomb did form,
But in our hearts, his spirit's warm.
Remember him, the tireless wheel,
Whose legacy, we'll always feel.

34. "From Sorrow to Triumph"

In mournful shadow, let my verses flow,
Where echoes of lament in whispers lie,
A sorrow deep, that only angels know,
Of love that chose to suffer and to die;
O broken heart, in grief you learn to fly.
The cross stands tall, where mercy met its end,
Yet through its pain, our souls begin to mend.
O sacred night, when darkness veiled the skies,
The world held breath as heaven's tears did fall,
And in the garden, hear those anguished cries,
The weight of sin upon Him, bearing all;
Each step He took towards that fateful call.
The burden great, yet love would not relent,
A sacrifice, divinely heaven-sent.
Behold the Lamb, in silence led away,
No word of protest, only love profound,
With every lash, our debts He did repay,
The thorns, the nails, the cross, His body crowned;
In death, His grace and mercy more renowned.
O bitter cup, O path of cruel fate,
For us He walked, through sorrow's narrow gate.
In quiet tomb, His lifeless body laid,

The world in mourning, hope seemed surely lost,
Yet through the silence, love would not be stayed,
A dawn would break, to melt the icy frost;
His victory sealed, no matter what the cost.
O heavy stone, soon rolled away in light,
For death could not hold Him, nor the night.
Awake, O soul, and see the risen King,
From sorrow's depths, to joy's eternal height,
With angels' choirs, let alleluias ring,
For in His triumph, darkness turns to light;
From death to life, He leads us through the night.
O radiant morn, where hope and glory blend,
In Christ, our Lord, our sorrows find their end.
O hearts once heavy, now with gladness filled,
The Savior lives, His love forever sure,
The wounds He bore, now healed and deeply stilled,
Our faith in Him, unshakable and pure;
In Him, our rest, our refuge to endure.
No more we mourn, as those who have no hope,
For through His cross, the gates of heaven open.
Eternal praise, our lips and lives shall give,
To Him who conquered death and sin for all,
In Him we move, and breathe, and truly live,
Responding to His sweet, compelling call;
With every tear, in joy we now recall.
O Savior dear, Your love our endless song,
In You we find where we, forever, belong.

35. The Silent Thief

How swiftly steals the silent thief of time,
With shadowed wings, he marks each fleeting year.
Though youth's bright dawn feels but a fleeting climb,
Its blossoms hide, replaced by autumn's tear.
The days, in haste, fly past with swift pursuit,
Yet spring's late bloom remains a distant dream.
For though the visage might seem firm and resolute,
The soul's deep roots lie far beneath the gleam.
Inward, the ripeness grows in measured pace,
Unlike the fortunate, who flourish soon.
Yet be it swift or slow, in time's embrace,
We walk our path beneath the watchful moon.
However humble, grand, or in between,
Each step is guided by a higher plan.
For in the eyes of Heaven's gaze serene,
Our every move is known, from first to span.
All lies within the grace we choose to wield,
As faithful stewards of the tasks we hold.
And in the Master's watch, our fate is sealed,
A story written in the stars, yet to unfold.

36. "Reflections in a Quiet Dell"

In a serene and verdant dell I find,
Amidst the rolling hills, a tranquil mind.
No songbird ever graced a stiller place,
No echo rang with more resplendent grace.
The heath-clad hills in silent grandeur stand,
Except that slope, adorned by Nature's hand,
Where golden gorse blooms ever bright and gay,
A vibrant canvas in the light of day.
The dell, kissed gently by the morning mist,
Is fresh as fields in early springtime kissed,
Its tender shoots like green translucent glass,
Through which the sun's soft evening glimmers pass.
Oh, what a quiet, spirit-soothing nook!
A place where one could read a sacred book,
Or lie on fern and heather, deeply still,
And drink the peace that solitude can fill.
Here might a humble soul, with heart contrite,
Find solace in the tranquil, golden light,
Reflect on youthful follies, bygone days,
Now wiser for life's unassuming ways.
The lark, unseen, sings high its joyous song,
A melody to which all peace belongs,

While gentle breezes, sun, and airy sky,
Bring healing whispers, tender as a sigh.
Such quiet contemplation brings to mind
A world at peace, with all mankind aligned.
Yet, sorrow stirs, as thoughts begin to roam
To distant lands, where conflicts fester, foam.
Beneath this sunlit peace, the hills could hide
The thunderous roar of war, its bloody tide.
O! Melancholy thought, that 'midst this grace,
Our brethren fight, their souls in direst place.
We, too, have erred, my countrymen, we've sinned,
Borne forth our vices on the tempest's wind.
Oppression's shadow cast on distant shores,
While we, at home, disdain what peace implores.
In Courts and Councils, all integrity,
Engulfed by greed, forsakes its purity.
The sacred words of faith, now muttered cold,
Proclaim the truths that few still dare to hold.
Yet, in this place, where Nature's voice is clear,
One might repent and shed each selfish tear.
O Britain, dear! O Mother Isle, so blessed,
May we, in truth, your sacred soil caress.
From every hill and vale, from sea to shore,
Let us emerge, with hearts made pure once more.
Reject the call of war, embrace the peace,
And let the cries of suffering souls decrease.
As twilight falls, the dell's perfume extends,
A golden scent the evening dew befriends.
The light retreats, the beacon fades from sight,

Yet still, the peaceful dell remains a light.
Farewell, sweet spot, I leave your quiet grace,
With heart renewed, to life's unhurried pace.
Ascending from the dell, I reach the crest,
And there, behold a vista richly blessed.
The rolling fields, the shadowed sea so wide,
The elms that guard my friend's abode with pride.
And hidden just beyond those stately trees,
My humble home, where love and joy find ease.
With steps now light, I hasten to my kin,
The silent dell a gentle peace within.
Refreshed by Nature's quiet, sacred spell,
My heart now yearns to love and serve as well.

37. The Dance of Shadows

In shadows cast by fleeting light we dwell,

Caught in the whispers of a cosmic jest,

Our essence dances on the edge of night,

In futile search for meaning and for rest.

If all we are is but a fleeting breath,

A spark that flickers in the vast unknown,

What purpose lies within our fleeting dreams?

What truth remains when all the stars have flown?

We weave our lives from threads of light and dark,

A tapestry of joy and whispered fears,

Each moment woven with a lover's touch,

Yet frail as mist dissolved by morning's tears.

Oh, Man, thou seeker of the boundless void,

A vessel set adrift on seas of time,

What solace can be found in hollow joys,

In tears that echo an unspoken rhyme?

Why do we dance beneath the phantom moon,

In step with shadows of our shadowed fate?

In laughter and in sorrow intertwined,

We find no answer, only contemplate.

Yet, in this paradox of light and shade,

Where dreams dissolve and hopes are born anew,

Perhaps the meaning lies within the dance,

In steps unplanned, and moments fleeting too.

For though our being's being is unsure,
And life a riddle wrapped in mystery,
Still in the dance of shadows we endure,
And find in every breath a chance to be.

38. The Abandoned Blossom

Unkind is he, who severs thee in haste,
Dear gentle rose, in morning's tender light,
Savors briefly thy perfume, pure and chaste,
Then leaves thee lonely, fading from his sight.
Oh, mournful symbol! Had I come your way
To see your velvet petals kissed by dawn,
I would have let you in the garden stay,
And watched you blossom till the day was gone.
Now in remorse I view your wilted hue,
And shed a tear as Memory softly weeps,
Reminding me of hearts that once were true,
Now lost to time, where endless sorrow sleeps.
Much like your bloom, fair rose, so bright and rare,
She shone with beauty none could quite compare.
Yet thoughtless hands took all she had to give,
And left her longing for the love denied;
He walked away, unheeding she should live,
A captive to his whims, then cast aside.
Oh, fleeting joys that swiftly fade away,
When will we learn to cherish while we may?

39. If Dreams Had Wings

If I could soar on gentle wings
And fly to where my heart is heard,
I'd swiftly come to you.
But dreams like these are fleeting things,
And I remain askew.
Yet in my dreams, to you I glide:
I'm always near when slumber calls,
Where love is truly free.
But morning breaks, and where do I reside?
In solitude's vast sea.
Though sleep may fade with morning's light,
I treasure waking just before the dawn:
For in those quiet moments,
Though night has taken flight,
Dreams linger, softly drawn.

40. To the Noiseless Sufferers

In shadows cast by gilded spires, they dwell,

Forgotten souls, where wealth and hardship swell.

Amidst the clamour of a bustling street,

Their silent plight remains a rhythmic beat.

O gentle eyes, so tired and resigned,

What dreams have flickered, faded from your mind?

Does hope, a faint and distant ember glow,

Or does despair, like night, upon you grow?

In alleys dark where sunlight dares not tread,

A fragile form, its spirit thinly fed.

Yet in your gaze, a spark of life remains,

A whispered plea beneath unspoken chains.

O child of sorrow, patient in your woe,

What tales of strife do your young years forego?

The weary sighs of those who toil unseen,

The fleeting joys that poverty has gleaned.

Amidst the rubble of a world so vast,

Your tiny heart holds echoes of the past.

Of dreams denied and futures yet unknown,

In silent strength, a courage all your own.

For who among the opulent and proud

Can claim the grace of those beneath the shroud?

In humble rags, a nobler spirit lies,

Than in the haughty gleam of affluent eyes.

Oh, that the world could see with vision clear,
The dignity in lives we hold so dear.
For in their struggles, we are bound as one,
A tapestry where every thread is spun.
Rise, gentle heart, let kindness be your guide,
For in your hands, the power to abide.
To lift the veil, to break the chains of pain,
To see each soul as worthy, and remain.
In fields of peace where equity shall reign,
And laughter dances free from every chain,
We'll walk together, hand in hand, as friends,
In unity, where every sorrow mends.

41. The Palette of Memory

A brush—a gentle whisper, soft,
It paints the scenes we hold,
A tapestry of moments lost
In hues both bright and bold.
The canvas of the mind expands
With strokes both wide and light,
Each memory in shifting strands
Alive with day and night.
The brush can smooth the sharpest edge
Of sorrow's aching past,
Or gently trace a cherished pledge
In colors meant to last.
Yet, with its bristles, it can stir
The shadows deep within,
A Specter from the depths to blur
The line of now and then.
Oh! If our days, so swift and bright,
Were painted pure and clear,
That every scene within our sight
Could welcome brush sincere.
Then contemplation, calm and true,
Would bring a gentle peace,
As age bestows a softer view,
And time's quick pace would cease.

Our hearts, like tranquil waters, still
Beneath the moon's embrace,
Reflect the light, the gentle thrill
Of life in all its grace.
And so, with brush in steady hand,
We craft the dreams we see,
A masterpiece of life unplanned,
Our own soul's tapestry.

42. "The Rebirth of Hope"

In shadows of sorrow, the mourner stands lone,
His heart a vast sea where the tempests have flown,
He weeps in the silence, the world unaware,
Of the echoes of love lost to the cold, bitter air.
The whispers of memory cling to his soul,
In the quiet of night, where the dark rivers roll.
He longs for a dawn that will break the despair,
To melt the chill grip of grief's lingering snare.
Yet beyond the gray veil, a promise is born,
In the hush of the night, awaits the bright morn.
Though winter of sorrow may hold him in sway,
A summer of light shall drive darkness away.
For beyond this brief moment, eternity lies,
In gardens where tears are wiped from all eyes.
Where love is immortal, untouched by time's hand,
And joy is a blossom that forever will stand.
So rest, gentle spirit, your anguish will cease,
In the haven of solace, you'll find your release.
For in the embrace of the infinite's grace,
All wounds shall be healed, and all losses replaced.

43. Embrace the End

In the dissonance of life's fleeting breath,
We find the ever-present shadow, death.
A constant, natural, looming in the sky,
Yet, it is life, not death, that makes us cry.
Why do we fear what's always been a part,
Of every ending, every start?
It's not the dark, the still, the cold,
But living's lost potential, untold.
The Stoics knew, as we must learn,
To face the fire and not to burn.
In death's embrace, we find the key,
To living life intentionally.
"You're going to die," the wise one said,
And with those words, new life was bred.
A shift in view, a call to act,
To live, to love, with nothing lacked.
The vastness of the universe,
Reminds us all, for better or worse,
That insignificance is freeing,
To be our fullest selves, all-seeing.
To know that we'll be dust again,
Brings not despair, but freedom's reign.
It's not "Why try?" but "Why not now?"
In life's grand scheme, we take a bow.

Close is the time, forget we will,
And close too, the world grows still.
But in this space, the time between,
We craft our lives, the great unseen.
We shape our days with purpose clear,
For death is near, yet we don't fear.
We live in ways that justify,
A life well-lived when time's goodbye.
So let us audit, let us ask,
If death would take, would this still last?
Do we engage with deep intent,
Or waste our time, our days misspent?
The mundane ebbs, the trivial flows,
But in our hearts, the purpose grows.
We steward life with mindful care,
So death becomes a thing most rare.
For in our living, fully met,
We find peace, with no regret.
Our fears dissolve and in their stead,
A life well-lived, a life well-spread.
As the seasons come and go,
So too do we, and this we know.
It's not the length, but how we live,
That marks the legacy we give.
So face the end with a steady heart,
For life and death are not apart.
They're woven threads, a single line,
In life's grand tapestry, divine.

44. The Ballet of Excellence

A quiet strength that guides our path,
Through comfort's sweet seduction,
A discipline to face our fears,
To rise beyond reduction.
For in the crucible of self,
Our truest test is laid,
Not measured by another's goals,
But by the progress made.
Surround yourself with those who strive,
With hearts that beat as yours,
Their excellence will call to you,
To open unseen doors.
Yet, even when the lane is clear,
And you run the race alone,
Remember, excellence is near,
In seeds you've always sown.
To craft a life in harmony,
With values deeply held,
Is to embrace a personal truth,
Where excellence is spelled.
For every day, a choice we make,
To give our best and more,
In how we live and what we seek,
Our spirits learn to soar.
So chase not shadows on the wall,
Nor seek another's light,
The path of excellence is yours,
In your own heart's sight.

45. The Mind's Key: A Journey Through Thought

In the labyrinth of thoughts, we find our place,
A dance of shadows in the mind's vast space,
Where fears and joys like phantoms intertwine,
Our thoughts, our guides, through time's relentless race.
Contentment's key is not in what we hold,
But in the way our thinking is controlled,
Not by the flux of relationships' tide,
But by the light within, our minds unfold.
Oh, how the quality of thought defines
The peace we seek, the clarity that shines,
In every twist and turn, the mind's embrace,
A realm where reason, over turmoil, pines.
We sculpt our world with every mindful breath,
Transcending fear, we conquer even death,
For Viktor Frankl, in the darkest night,
Found freedom's flame within his spirit's depth.
To challenge thinking, not just to agree,
To seek the truth, to let assumptions flee,
Is labor's gift, a journey we embark,
Where clarity and wisdom both run free.
Not overthinking, lost in anxious storm,
Nor passive thought, where dangers subtly form,

But balanced, purposeful, a steady gaze,
Through trials and joy, through uniform and norm.
In every thought refined, a chance to grow,
To see the world in its unyielding flow,
For what we feel is shaped by what we think,
In every high, in every weighted low.
So let us harness thought with gentle might,
To find our way through darkness into light,
For in our minds, we hold the truest key,
To live with grace, with wisdom shining bright.
In moments still, where chaos does abound,
We find our strength, our feet upon the ground,
With every thought, a choice to rise or fall,
We shape our lives, in thinking, we are crowned.

46. Nature's Threads

In Nature's woven strands, each life a tale to tell,
For ages, we have claimed we're grand, the peak where beings' dwell.
With mind and craft, we've grown in pride, believing we're supreme,
Yet mysteries abound, much more than we can dream.
Seeing all as ours to rule, with beings at our heel,
Taking all Earth's treasures, thinking conquest seals the deal.
Warnings often go unheard, a wiser voice we miss,
That we are part of Nature, not a force to dismiss.
Nature holds a power vast, in storms and droughts and fire,
In unseen battles raging, microbes' forms inspire.
In air and soil and water, tiny lives abound,
In fierce, unseen arenas, their destinies are found.
Within us too, they flourish, a host of life unseen,
A myriad of tiny forms, in complex balance keen.
Their presence crucial to our health, a gift we must defend,
In harmony's fine dance, on them we do depend.
Animals, too, bear Nature's might, with creatures small and great,
Diseases rise in shadowed ways, a heavy toll we fate.
From forests lost to urban sprawl, new threats begin to creep,
A reminder stark and clear, for heedless ways we keep.
As trees fall and lands transform, new contacts do we face,
Climate shifts and warming lands, new vectors find their place.
Biting pests with fevered sting, in warmer climes they thrive,
Spreading fear and illness wide, as seasons change, they drive.

Diverse forms once held in check, now rise in empty space,

As ecosystems crumble, new plagues we must embrace.

From hidden depths and shaded woods, new threats emerge to loom,

In balance lost, new dangers born, to fill the empty room.

Unseen foes in broken lands, diseases find their way,

In altered habitats, they rise, and with them, so do we sway.

Yet often do we falter, forgetting Nature's might,

Until her force awakens, to set our wrongs to right.

Recent times a lesson teach, a warning we must heed,

In whispered tones, Nature speaks, of change and urgent need.

To heal the wounds we've wrought, a distance must we learn,

A shift in ways and thoughts, for balance to return.

A path of care and wisdom, a way to tread anew,

To lessen risk, to give our care, in all we say and do.

In Nature's web, each thread is dear, with tender hands we mend,

Respecting ancient rhythms, our shared world to defend.

47. In the Twilight of Youth

In the twilight of youth, where shadows dance,
Where innocence holds its fragile stance,
Teens wander through a labyrinth of choice,
Voices of freedom, yet a deceptive voice.
They feel invincible, with stars in their eyes,
Unaware of the storm behind the guise,
Each sip of drink, each puff of smoke,
A thread in the fabric of dreams that broke.
A fleeting escape, a temporary thrill,
Yet beneath it lies a void, a silent ill,
For the path they tread is tangled and steep,
In the web of addiction, secrets they keep.
A family history, a heart that's been bruised,
A soul that feels lost, by the world misused,
Depression's cold grip, low self-esteem's cry,
In the fog of confusion, they reach for the sky.
In shadows of friends, with pills and with powders,
They seek solace in fleeting, hollow towers,
Yet the dangers loom large, like Specters of night,
Turning moments of joy into endless fright.
Physical tolls, from health to the soul,
Emotional storms take their heavy toll,
Family bonds fray, like threads in the dark,
As schoolwork crumbles, and ignites a stark.

New friends in the alley, where choices are slim,
Dress and music in shadows grow dim,
Unseen dangers lurk, like ghosts in the hall,
Yet signs can be missed in the rush of it all.
Parents must guide through the turbulent sea,
With open hearts and a vigilant plea,
Speak with compassion, lead with the light,
Secure the safe harbor through the dark of the night.
For each choice made in the young twilight's haze,
Can shape the journey through life's complex maze,
In the dance of the shadows, let wisdom prevail,
Guiding young souls through the storm and the gale.

48. "Echoes of Choice and Causation"

In the labyrinth of mind and soul's embrace,
Freedom and Determinism waltz in a tangled grace.
Is man the sculptor, chisel in hand,
Or a mere clay, shaped by fate's command?
Freedom, a beacon, bold and bright,
Guides us through the darkest night.
Choice and chance in every breath,
Moral paths where truth and myth both sets.
Yet Determinism whispers through the breeze,
A chain of cause, a web that never frees.
Natural law and the divine's grand scheme,
Actions are echoes of a cosmic dream.
Hard determinists see no liberty,
In a world where fate writes every plea.
"Liberty of indifference," they say,
Is but an illusion, a fleeting ray.
Soft determinists find a middle road,
Where choice blooms from a pre-written code.
"Liberty of Spontaneity," they claim,
A dance within the universe's frame.
Libertarians dream of skies unbound,
Where freedom reigns, where choices resound.

Determinism's shadows fade away,
In the light of human will's bright day.
Yet, in this conflict, a truth does lie,
Freedom and Determinism in a cosmic tie.
One's heart may hold the key to both,
Balancing belief with reason's oath.
So, in this dance of freedom and fate,
We choose our steps; we seal our state.
Whether as sculptors or clay we stand,
Both paths converge in the soul's grand band.

49. The Quest for Truth

In quest of truth, belief we hold,
A quest as ancient as tales of old.
To know the world, our hearts aspire,
To match our minds with truth's pure fire.
Belief, a step upon this road,
A bridge to knowledge, though not its abode.
For truth must anchor belief's flight,
Or else it fades into the night.
True beliefs, a treasure sought,
In webs of thought and lessons taught.
False beliefs, a shadow cast,
From errors made in moments past.
Our minds reach out to grasp the real,
Through layers of the world's appeal.
We seek a match, a harmony,
Between our thoughts and what must be.
Objective truth, the cornerstone,
In realms of fact, it's truth alone.
For in its light, knowledge blooms,
And falsehoods fade, consumed in gloom.
Some may claim truth's but a guise,
Relativism's shifting skies.
Yet in our hearts, a fire burns bright,
To find what's real in darkest night.

If beauty's but the beholder's sight,
Its truth eludes our seeking light.
Yet in the quest for what we know,
In fact's firm ground, our roots must grow.
So let us seek with hearts sincere,
Through doubt and wonder, hope and fear.
For knowledge stands where truth is found,
In minds where true beliefs are crowned.

50. The Vanities of Existence

In the quiet dawn of morning's light,
A man awakens from the night,
To melancholy's subtle might,
A nameless dread, an endless fight.
He gazes at the boundless skies,
Where time and space before him lies,
In their vastness, he's but a sigh,
A fleeting breath, a question why.
The world around him, cold and bare,
With truths exiled, and falsehoods fair,
A social mask we're taught to wear,
Where beauty hides in dark despair.
He sees injustice, feels the pain,
Of culture's loss and apathy's reign,
A world obsessed with wealth and gain,
Where deeper yearnings seem in vain.
The days grow dark, the months grow long,
His heart beats to a mournful song,
He wonders if he's right or wrong,
In feeling that he doesn't belong.
Depression, some might claim, is ill,
A malady to treat with pills,
To quiet thoughts and calm the will,
And bend the mind to fit the bill.

But what if, in this state of woe,
There lies a truth we rarely know,
A wisdom that begins to grow,
Where deeper meanings start to show?
Philosophers of days gone by,
Have pondered life with a discerning eye,
Schopenhauer's despairing cry,
And Laing's quest to seek the why.
In genius, too, the shadows fall,
Poe's raven haunts, Nietzsche's call,
Van Gogh's colors, Plath's dark pall,
A brilliance shines beyond the wall.
Perhaps the sorrow that we face,
Is not a curse, but a saving grace,
A call to see the human race,
In a new and unaccustomed place.
To question norms and seek the truth,
To find in age what's lost in youth,
To recognize the wisdom's proof,
That life is more than surface sleuth.
For in the depths of dark despair,
A flame of insight starts to flare,
A vision of the world laid bare,
Where meaning's found in self-aware.
So let us not, in haste, prescribe,
A drug to mask, a norm to bribe,
But seek the depths where sorrows bribe,
And find the truths that therein hide.
For in the melancholy's grip,

The soul embarks on a profound trip,
Where truths and beauty often slip,
And life's true essence starts to sip.
In understanding, let's confide,
That depression, far from being denied,
May be the path where wisdom's tried,
A guide where deeper meanings hide.

Conclusion

As you reach the conclusion of this poetry collection, I hope that the words you've encountered have resonated with you on a deep and personal level. Poetry has the unique ability to evoke emotions, provoke thought, and create connections that transcend the boundaries of time and space. It is my sincere wish that these poems have offered you moments of reflection, solace, and inspiration.

In the course of writing these poems, I have sought to explore the intricate layers of the human experience—our joys, sorrows, hopes, and fears. Through themes of love, solitude, nature, and spiritual devotion, I have aimed to capture the essence of what it means to be human, to live and to feel, and to search for meaning in a complex world.

This collection is not an end but a beginning—a starting point for further reflection, discussion, and personal growth. The themes explored here are timeless and universal, yet each reader will find their own unique meaning within the verses. I encourage you to revisit these poems, to let them speak to you in different ways over time, and to find new insights with each reading.

As we part ways at the close of this book, I want to express my deepest gratitude for your time and attention. It is the reader who gives life to the words on these pages, who completes the circle of communication that poetry seeks to establish. Your engagement with this collection is what makes it truly meaningful.

If these poems have touched you, challenged you, or inspired you in any way, then my purpose as a poet has been fulfilled. Poetry is a living art form, one that grows and evolves with each reader, and I am honored to have shared this journey with you.

Thank you for allowing these words into your life. May they continue to inspire, comfort, and guide you long after you have turned the final page.

With warm regards and sincere appreciation,

Dr. Jipson Lawrance J.